About the Author

Paul Watson is a technology enthusiast and has got massive experience in various technologies like web application development, automation testing, build automation, continuous integration and deployment technologies. He has worked on most of the technology stacks.

He has hands on experience on UFT, LeanFT, Selenium and Appium. He has used testing frameworks like JUnit, TestNG, Cucumber with Selenium. He has also worked on Struts, Spring, Bootstratp, Angular JS.

His hobbies include travelling to new tourist places, watching basketball, tennis and learning latest technological stuff.

A special note of thanks to my Wife

I would like to dedicate this book to my lovely wife for loving me so much and helping me write this book. Without her support, this book would not have been a reality.

Who this book is for

This book is for automation engineers who want to learn Selenium in Node.js to automate the web applications.

It is assumed that reader has basic programming skills in JavaScript language. Whether you are a beginner or an experienced developer, this book will help you master the skills on Selenium in Node.js.

The book starts with introduction of Selenium and then dives into key concepts as mentioned below.

1. Launching browsers with Desired Capabilities – Chrome, Chrome with options, Chrome in Mobile Emulation, IE, Firefox
2. Element Identification – Element identification methods, Advanced XPATH expressions, Advanced CSS selectors
3. Assertions in Selenium in Node.js
4. Interacting with elements in Selenium in Node.js
5. Basic Browser window automation
6. Sending keys in Selenium in Node.js
7. Synchronization in Selenium
8. Check if Element exists
9. Working with Tables using Selenium
10. Performing advanced actions using Selenium in Node.js
11. Executing JavaScript in Selenium in Node.js
12. Switching contexts – Working with multiple Browser Windows or tabs, Working with multiple frames, Handling alerts

13. Common exceptions in Selenium
14. Frameworks in Selenium – Taking a screenshot in selenium, Mocha – Unit testing framework
15. Selenium grid

Table of Contents

1. Introduction to Selenium Webdriver

Selenium Webdriver is the industry leading web automation testing tool.

Main features of Selenium are given below.

1. Open source
2. Cross platform
3. Automates all major browsers like Internet Explorer, Microsoft edge, Google chrome, Firefox, Safari, Opera
4. We can write the tests in various languages like Java, Groovy, C#.Net, VB.Net, Node.js, PHP, Python, Ruby, Perl, objective C and many more!
5. Runs on JSON webdriver protocol over HTTP

Below image shows how the Selenium Webdriver protocol works.

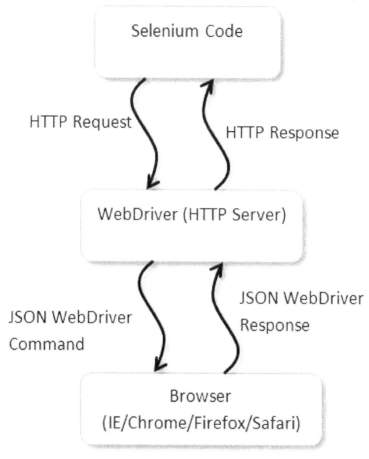

Selenium Webdriver Protocol

2. Introduction to Node.js

Node.js is used to develop server side web applications using JavaScript. Node.js is a javascript run time environment. Node.js basically runs a javascript code. Node.js has an event driven architecture. Most of the methods are asynchronous.

Key features of Node.js

1. Open source
2. Cross platform
3. Runs on Google's V8 Javascript engine used in chrome browser
4. Allows you to execute Javascript on server
5. Uses event driven programming
6. NPM is used a package manager in Node.js

Editors for Nodejs

1. We can use the editors like visual studio, eclipse, Intellij etc to develop Node.js applications.
2. You can also develop the code in simple notepad or notepad++.

Node.js runs on single thread. Then obvious question you may ask is how it can support multiple requests? The main point here is that even though node.js runs on single thread, all requests are handled in asynchronous manner.

For example - let us say we want to do 2 tasks
task1 - Read a file1
task2 - Write file2

As long as requests are not dependent on each other, Node.js will register a call back for both tasks. Both tasks will start running and whenever any of the task completion event occurs, node.js will invoke the call back function. When you use node.js as a server, this event loop never ends.

In synchronous approach, task2 will be blocked until task1 finishes.
But in asynchronous approach(node.js), task2 will not be blocked. Both tasks will be running in parallel. Both tasks register call back if any. At the end of the task completion, those call back methods are invoked.

What if task2 depends on task1?
In this case, you can use promises and Fibers

3. Installation and Environment set up

You need to follow below steps to set up the environment for running Selenium tests using Node.js

1. Download and install Node.js
2. Install Selenium Webdriver package for Node.js
3. Download the drivers for various browsers like IE, Chrome, Firefox etc
4. Write the tests in Java Script and Execute it.

<u>Downloading and Installing Node.js</u>

Just visit official Node.js website(https://nodejs.org/en/) and download the Node.js installer for windows. Double click on that installer file and follow on-screen instructions to install the Node.js. After installation is completed, update the system path to include the location of Node.js installation directory.

Node.js in System Path

To ensure that Node.js is installed correctly, open the command prompt and execute below command.

Checking Node.js Version

As you can see, I have got v4.4.7 installed on my system.

Installing Selenium Webdriver Package for Node.js

Next you have to install the Selenium Webdriver package for Node.js. For that, just execute below command in a command prompt.

npm install selenium-webdriver

Downloading driver files for browsers

After that download the driver applications for each browsers and update the system path to point to the location where you have placed the drivers.

1. http://chromedriver.storage.googleapis.com/index .html
2. http://selenium-release.storage.googleapis.com/index.html
3. http://go.microsoft.com/fwlink/?LinkId=619687
4. https://github.com/mozilla/geckodriver/releases/
5. http://selenium-release.storage.googleapis.com/index.html

I have put the chromedriver.exe and IEDriverServer.exe files in Downloads directory so I have updated the path variable as shown in below image.

Driver files included in System Path

12

Writing and running the first script using Node.js

Then write the sample selenium code as shown in below example and save the file as launchChrome.js

```
var webdriver = require('selenium-webdriver');

var driver = new webdriver.Builder()
        .forBrowser('chrome')
        .build();

    driver.get('http://www.softpost.org');
    driver.quit();
```

To execute the above file, you need to fire below command in a command prompt.

node launchChrome.js

There are many Node.js packages out there for browser automation using Selenium. But we we would be using selenium-webdriver official package.

Here is the list of other node.js packages for selenium automation.

1. Synchronized Selenium Webdriver -
   https://www.npmjs.com/package/webdriver-sync
2. Another way is by using node-fibers and wd-synch libraries as explained at Webdriver.io

4. NPM - Package Manage for Node.js

NPM is a package manager for Node.js
(https://www.npmjs.com/)is the official website of NPM.

We can use NPM to do below things.

1. List Node.js packages
2. Search Node.js packages
3. Uninstall Node.js packages
4. Update Node.js packages

NPM uses package.json file to manage the packages
dependencies.

Below command will list all downloaded packages.
npm ls

To install any package, you have to use below command.

```
npm install <package-name>
```

npm install selenium-webdriver
Use below commands to set up node.js project locally.

```
npm init
```

package.json file contains all project information like main
module file, name of the module, project url, authors etc.
If you are behind the proxy, you will need to configure the
proxy server as shown in below command.
npm config set proxy
http://user:pass@proxyserevr:proxyport

5. Directory layout of Selenium Webdriver Node.js package

When you install the selenium-webdriver package, selenium-webdriver directory is created in node_modules.

index.js is the main file of selenium-webdriver package.

Below things are exported from index.js of selenium-webdriver package.

1. exports.ActionSequence = actions.ActionSequence;
2. exports.Browser = capabilities.Browser;
3. exports.Builder = Builder;
4. exports.Button = input.Button;
5. exports.By = by.By;
6. exports.Capabilities = capabilities.Capabilities;
7. exports.Capability = capabilities.Capability;
8. exports.Condition = webdriver.Condition;
9. exports.EventEmitter = events.EventEmitter;
10. exports.FileDetector = input.FileDetector;
11. exports.Key = input.Key;
12. exports.Session = session.Session;
13. exports.WebDriver = webdriver.WebDriver;
14. exports.WebElement = webdriver.WebElement;
15. exports.WebElementCondition = webdriver.WebElementCondition;
16. exports.WebElementPromise = webdriver.WebElementPromise;
17. exports.error = error;
18. exports.logging = logging;
19. exports.promise = promise;
20. exports.until = until;

selenium-webdriver/lib directory contains important modules like webdriver, actions, by etc.

Below things are exported from selenium-webdriver/lib/webdriver.js

1. Alert: Alert
2. AlertPromise: AlertPromise
3. Condition: Condition
4. Logs: Logs
5. Navigation: Navigation
6. Options: Options
7. TargetLocator: TargetLocator
8. Timeouts: Timeouts
9. WebDriver: WebDriver
10. WebElement: WebElement
11. WebElementCondition: WebElementCondition
12. WebElementPromise: WebElementPromise
13. Window: Window

6. Launching browsers with Desired Capabilities

6.1 Launch chrome using selenium in Node.js

Here is the sample code to launch the chrome browser using Node.js

```
var webdriver = require('selenium-webdriver');

var driver = new webdriver.Builder()
.forBrowser('chrome')
.build();

driver.get('http://www.softpost.org');
driver.quit();
```

Save above file with name s1.js

To run above code, you can use below command.

```
node s1.js
```

6.2 Launching the chrome browser with chrome options

Here is the sample code to launch the chrome browser with chrome options

```
var assert = require('assert');
var webdriver = require('selenium-webdriver'),
By = webdriver.By,
until = webdriver.until;

var chrome = require("selenium-
webdriver/chrome");

var options = new chrome.Options();
```

```
//Start browser using below binary file
//options.setChromeBinaryPath(pathToChromeBinar
y);

//Start browser in Maximized mode using below option
options.addArguments("start-maximized");

//Disable pop ups using below option
options.addArguments("disable-popup-blocking");

//disable developer extension using below option
options.addArguments("chrome.switches","--
disable-extensions");

//security warning is disabled using below option
options.addArguments("test-type");


var driver = new webdriver.Builder().
withCapabilities(options.toCapabilities()).buil
d();


driver.get("http://www.softpost.org");
driver.close();
driver.quit();
```

6.3 Chrome in Mobile Emulation

Chrome driver allows you to test your web application on emulated mobile devices(Android and iOS).

Below example illustrates how to launch chrome in Mobile Emulation using Selenium in Node.js

```javascript
var assert = require('assert');
var webdriver = require('selenium-webdriver'),
By = webdriver.By,
until = webdriver.until;


var chrome = require("selenium-
webdriver/chrome");

//Below code snippet shows how to launch chrome with
mobile emulation mode.
var driver = new webdriver.Builder()
.forBrowser('chrome')
.setChromeOptions(new chrome.Options()
.setMobileEmulation({deviceName: 'Apple iPhone
5'})
//.setMobileEmulation({deviceName: 'Google
Nexus 5'})
//.setMobileEmulation({deviceName: 'Google
Nexus 7'})
.addArguments("start-maximized")
.addArguments("test-type")
)
.build();

//Rest of the operations will be done in emulation
mode
driver.get('http://www.softpost.org/selenium-
test-page/');

driver.quit();
```

6.4 Launching IE browser using Node.js

Here is the sample code to automate the IE browser using Node.js

```
var webdriver = require('selenium-webdriver');

//create shortcuts for By and until classes
By = webdriver.By,
until = webdriver.until;

var driver = new webdriver.Builder()
.forBrowser('ie')
.build();

driver.get('http://www.softpost.org');
driver.quit();
```

We can also run the tests on different browsers using below syntax

```
SELENIUM_BROWSER=chrome node myscript.js

SELENIUM_BROWSER=safari node myscript.js
```

6.5 Launch the firefox browser

Here is the sample code to launch the firefox browser using Node.js

```
var webdriver = require('selenium-webdriver');


var driver = new webdriver.Builder()
.forBrowser('firefox')
.build();


driver.get('http://www.softpost.org');
driver.close();
driver.quit();
```

You should have geckodriver in your PATH for firefox 47.0.1 onwards

You may get below error on windows 64 if you use 64 bit Geckodriver. To fix that error, use 32 bit driver.

```
WebDriverError: Unable to parse new session
response: {"error":"unknown error","
message":"Expected browser binary location, but
unable to find binary in default
location, no 'moz:firefoxOptions.binary'
capability provided, and no binary flag set on
the command line"}
```

7. Element Identification

7.1 Element identification methods

We can identify the web elements using below Element locators in Node.js

1. className
2. tagName
3. name
4. id
5. xpath
6. css
7. linkText
8. partialLinkText

Here are some of the examples that illustrate how to identify elements in Node.js

```
driver.findElement(By.className('myclassName'))
.sendKeys('watson');
driver.findElement(By.tagName('input')).sendKey
s('watson');
driver.findElement(By.name('fname')).sendKeys('
watson');
driver.findElement(By.id('myid')).sendKeys('wat
son');
driver.findElement(By.xpath('//input[@name='fna
me']')).sendKeys('watson');
driver.findElement(By.css('input[name='fname']'
)).sendKeys('watson');
driver.findElement(By.linkText('Home')).click()
;
driver.findElement(By.partialLintText('me')).cl
ick();
```

Selenium webdriver with Node.js

findElements method returns array of elements.

This method returns all elements matching given locator.

Here is an example on findElements method

```
var webdriver = require('selenium-webdriver');
//create shortcuts for By and until classes

By = webdriver.By,
until = webdriver.until;
var driver = new webdriver.Builder()
.forBrowser('chrome')
.build();

driver.get('http://www.softpost.org');

var webElements =
driver.findElements(By.partialLinkText("torial"
));

webElements.then(function (elements) {

//Work on each element
for (var i=0; i < elements.length; i++){
elements[i].getText().then(function(txt){
console.log(txt + "\n");
});
}
});

//close the browser

driver.close();

driver.quit();
```

7.2 Advanced XPATH expressions

What is xpath in selenium web driver?

xpath is used to find the specific element in the given webpage.

Some of the below examples will demonstrate how we can write the xpath expressions.

Find all elements with tag input	//input
Find all input tag element having attribut e type = 'hidden'	//input[@type='hidden']
Find all input tag element having attribut e type = 'hidden' and name attribute = 'ren'	//input[@type='hidden'][@name='ren']
Find all input tag element with attribute type containing	//input[contains(@type,'hid')]

'hid'	
Find all input tag element with attribute type starting with 'hid'	//input[starts-with(@type,'hid')]
Find all elements having innertext = 'password'	//*[text()='Password']
Find all td elements having innertext = 'password'	//td[text()='Password']
Find all next siblings of td tag having innertext = 'gender'	//td[text()='Gender']//following-sibling::*
Find all elements in the 2nd next sibling of td tag having innertext =	//td[text()='Gender']//following-sibling::*[2]//*

'gender'	
Find input elements in the 2nd next sibling of td tag having innertext = 'gender'	//td[text()='Gender']//following-sibling::*[2]//input
Find the td which contains font element containing the text '12'	//td[font[contains(text(),'12')]]
Find all the preceding siblings of the td which contains font element containing the text '12'	//td[font[contains(text(),'12')]]//preceding-sibling::*
Find the second td ancestor of the span element containing text - Exp Date then find the	//span[text()='Exp Date']//ancestor::td[2]//preceding-sibling::td

previous td element'	
Find the first td ancestor of the span element containing text - Exp Date then find the previous td element	//span[text()='Exp Date']//ancestor::td[1]//preceding-sibling::td
Find the element containing specific text	//p[text()[contains(.,'refer')]]

Below example shows how to use logical operators (and / or / not) in XPATH.

```
//div[contains(@class,'result-row') and not
(contains(@style,'none'))]
```

Below example shows how to handle the quote inside text

```
//label[contains(text(),"Killer\'s age.")]
```

7.3 Advanced CSS selectors

What is CssSelector in selenium web driver?

cssSelector is used to find the specific element in the given webpage.

Some of the below examples will demonstrate how we can write the cssSelector expressions.

Find all elements with tag input	input
Find all input tag element having attribute type = 'hidden'	input[type='hidden']
Find all input tag element having attribute type = 'hidden' and name attribute = 'ren'	input[type='hidden'][name='ren']
Find all input tag element with attribute type containing 'hid'	input[type*='hid']
Find all input tag element with attribute type	input[type^='hid']

starting with 'hid'	
Find all input tag element with attribute type ending with 'den'	input[type$='den']

You can find the element containing specific text using below CSS Selector syntax.

```
$("h3:contains('Cloud')")
```

Above css will select the element H3 containing text Cloud

8. Assertions in Selenium in Node.js

We would be using built in Assertion library in node.js

Below code snippet shows how to use built-in assert module in Node.js

```
var assert = require('assert');
```

Below assertion will pass if the first argument is true

```
assert(value[, message])
assert(1==1,"Check that 2 values are equal");
```

Below assertion functions are used to verify that 2 variables contains same data or not.

```
assert.equal(actual, expected[, message])
assert.notEqual(actual, expected[, message])
```

Below assertion functions are used to verify that 2 variables contains same data or not. 2 Objects are strictly equal when they refer to the same object.

```
assert.strictEqual(actual, expected[, message])
assert.notStrictEqual(actual, expected[,
message])
```

Below assertion functions are used to verify that 2 variables contains same data or not recursively. This is useful in comparing the JSON objects.

```
assert.deepEqual(actual, expected[, message])
assert.notDeepEqual(actual, expected[,
message])
```

Below assertion functions are used to verify that 2 variables contains same data or not recursively and strictly.

```
assert.deepStrictEqual(actual, expected[,
message])
assert.notDeepStrictEqual(actual, expected[,
message])
```

Below assertion will pass if the exception is thrown in the code block.

```
assert.throws(block[, error][, message])
assert.doesNotThrow(block[, error][, message])
```

We would be using promises to add the sync points.

There are many other third party assertion libraries available in Node.js

So you can use any of them.

1. should.js
2. expect.js
3. chai
4. better-assert
5. unexpected

Below example shows how you can add the assertions in the test.

```
var assert = require('assert');
var webdriver = require('selenium-webdriver'),
By = webdriver.By,
until = webdriver.until;
```

```
var driver = new webdriver.Builder()
.forBrowser('chrome')
.build();

driver.get('http://www.softpost.org/selenium-
test-page/');

driver.getTitle().then(function(title) {
console.log("title is " + title);

//Below assertion is successful as the title
contains substring - selenium test page
assert(title.toLowerCase().indexOf("selenium
test page")!==1);
});

/* Here is an alternative syntax to write
promises.
var promise = driver.getTitle();

promise.then(function(title) {
console.log("title is " + title);
});
*/

driver.quit();
```

9. Interacting with elements in Selenium in Node.js

Below example illustrates how to interact with elements in Selenium in Node.js

```
var assert = require('assert');
var webdriver = require('selenium-webdriver'),
By = webdriver.By,
until = webdriver.until;


var chrome = require("selenium-
webdriver/chrome");


var options = new chrome.Options();
options.addArguments("start-maximized");
options.addArguments("test-type");
var driver = new webdriver.Builder().
withCapabilities(options.toCapabilities()).buil
d();


driver.get('http://www.softpost.org/selenium-
test-page/');
```

Setting data

To set the data in editbox, you can use below syntax.

```
driver.findElement(By.id("myeditboxid")).sendKe
ys("hi");
```

To select or unselect the checkbox, radiobuttons, you can use below syntax.

```
driver.findElement(By.id("mycheckboxid")).click
();
```

33

To submit the form, use below method.

```
submit()
driver.submit().then(function() {
console.log("Form is submitted");
});
```

To clear the data from input box, use below method.

```
clear()

driver.findElement(By.id("myid")).clear().then(
function() {
console.log("myid is cleared");
});
```

Sending keys

```
driver.findElement(By.id('fn')).sendKeys('Shaun
');

driver.findElement(By.id('fn')).getAttribute('v
alue').then(function(value) {
console.log("First value entered in edit box ->
" + value);
assert(value=='Shaun');
});

driver.findElement(By.id('fn')).clear();
driver.findElement(By.id('fn')).sendKeys('Hyden
');

driver.findElement(By.xpath("//input[@value='QT
P']")).click();
```

```
//Below statement will force driver to wait for
5 seconds before performing next actions
driver.sleep(5000);
```

Reading data from page

To get css value of an element , use below method.

```
getCssValue()

driver.findElement(By.id("myid")).getCssValue('
width').then(function(value) {
console.log("Width is " + value);
});
```

To get tag name of an element , use below method.

```
getTagName()

driver.findElement(By.linkText("Open New
Window")).getTagName().then(function(value) {
console.log("TagName is " + value);
});
```

To get value of an attribute of an element, use below method.

```
getAttribute(attributeName)

driver.findElement(By.id("myid")).getAttribute(
'class').then(function(value) {
console.log("Class value is " + value);
});
```

```
To get inner text of an element, use below
method.
driver.findElement(By.id("myid")).getText().the
n(function(value) {
console.log("Text is " + value);
});
```

To check if an element is enabled or not, use below
method.

```
isEnabled()

driver.findElement(By.id("myid")).isEnabled().t
hen(function(value) {
console.log("is myid enabled? " + value);
});
```

To check if an checkbox or radio button is selected or not,
use below method.

```
isSelected()

driver.findElement(By.id("myid")).isSelected().
then(function(value) {
console.log("is myid selected? " + value);
});
```

To check if an element is displayed or not, use below
method.

```
isDisplayed()
driver.findElement(By.id("myid")).isDisplayed()
.then(function(value) {
console.log("myid is displayed?" + value);
});
```

```
driver.findElement(By.id('fn')).isEnabled().the
n(function(value) {
console.log("First name edit box is enabled? ->
" + value);
assert(value==true);
});


driver.findElement(By.xpath("//input[@value='QT
P']")).isSelected().then(function(value) {
console.log("QTP checkbox is selected?-> " +
value);
assert(value==true);
});


driver.findElement(By.tagName("p")).getText().t
hen(function(txt) {
console.log("Text in first paragraph -> " +
txt);
assert(txt.toLowerCase().indexOf("selenium") >
0);
});
driver.findElement(By.xpath("//input[@value='QT
P']")).getTagName().then(function(value) {
console.log("tag name of QTP checkbox is -> " +
value);
assert(value=="input");
});
driver.findElement(By.xpath("//input[@value='Si
gn up']")).isDisplayed().then(function(value) {
console.log("is Sign up button displayed? -> "
+ value);
assert(value==true);
});


driver.sleep(5000);
driver.quit();
```

10 . Basic Browser window automation
Below example illustrates how to automate below things using Selenium Webdriver in Node.js

1. Navigate back and forward
2. Maximizing the browser window
3. Resizing the window
4. Getting the title of current web page
5. Getting the url of current page
6. Getting the HTML source of current page

```
var assert = require('assert');
var webdriver = require('selenium-webdriver'),
By = webdriver.By,
until = webdriver.until;


var chrome = require("selenium-
webdriver/chrome");


var options = new chrome.Options();
options.addArguments("start-maximized");
options.addArguments("disable-popup-blocking");
options.addArguments("test-type");
var driver = new webdriver.Builder().
withCapabilities(options.toCapabilities()).buil
d();


driver.get('http://www.softpost.org/selenium-
test-page/');
driver.get('http://www.softpost.org');


//We can use below code to navigate forward and
backward.
driver.navigate().back();
```

```
driver.sleep(4000);
driver.navigate().forward();


//You can maximize the browser windows using below
code.
driver.manage().window().maximize();


//You can set the window size using below code.
driver.manage().window().setSize(200,200);


//Below code shows how you can get the title of web
page.
driver.get('http://www.softpost.org/selenium-
test-page/');
driver.getTitle().then(function(title) {
console.log("title is " + title);
assert(title=='Selenium Test Page | Free
Software Tutorials');
});
//Below code shows alternative syntax to use
promises in Node.js
var promise = driver.getTitle();
promise.then(function(title) {
console.log("title is " + title);
});


//To get current url, use getCurrentUrl() method.
driver.getCurrentUrl().then(function(url) {
console.log("Url is " + url);
});


//To get html source of current page, use
getPageSource() method.
driver.getPageSource().then(function(source) {
console.log("Page source is " + source);
});


driver.quit();
```

Sending keys in Selenium in Node.js

Below example illustrates how to send keys in Selenium in Node.js

```
var assert = require('assert');
var webdriver = require('selenium-webdriver'),
By = webdriver.By,
until = webdriver.until;


var chrome = require("selenium-
webdriver/chrome");


var options = new chrome.Options();
options.addArguments("start-maximized");
options.addArguments("disable-popup-blocking");
options.addArguments("test-type");
var driver = new webdriver.Builder().
withCapabilities(options.toCapabilities()).buil
d();


driver.get('http://www.softpost.org/selenium-
test-page/');


//You can use below code to send the keys to elements.


driver.findElement(By.id("fn")).sendKeys("Shaun
" + webdriver.Key.ENTER);
driver.findElement(By.id("fn")).sendKeys(webdri
ver.Key.chord(webdriver.Key.CONTROL, "a"));


driver.sleep(4000);


driver.quit();
```

11. Synchronization in Selenium, Check if Element exists

We can have 3 types of timeouts.

1. pageLoadTimeout
2. implicitlyWait
3. explicit wait

Below line of code shows how to set page load timeout

```
driver.manage().timeouts().pageLoadTimeout(50,T
imeUnit.SECONDS);
```

Below line of code shows how to set implicit wait timeout

```
driver.manage().timeouts().implicitlyWait(20,
TimeUnit.SECONDS);
```

Below line of code shows explicit wait timeout syntax.

```
driver.wait(condition, optional_timeout,
optional_message)
```

For example - If you want to wait until title of the page becomes say "Selenium Test Page", you can use below syntax.

```
driver.wait(until.titleIs('Selenium Test
Page'), 1000);
```

Here are all of the wait conditions that you can use in your scripts.

1. ableToSwitchToFrame(frame)
2. attemptToSwitchFrames(driver, frame)
3. alertIsPresent()
4. titleIs(title)
5. titleContains(substr)
6. titleMatches(regex)
7. urlIs(url)
8. urlContains(substrUrl)
9. function urlMatches(regex)
10. elementLocated(locator)
11. elementsLocated(locator)
12. stalenessOf(element)
13. elementIsVisible(element)
14. elementIsNotVisible(element)
15. elementIsEnabled(element)
16. elementIsDisabled(element)
17. elementIsSelected(element)
18. elementIsNotSelected(element)
19. elementTextIs(element, text)
20. elementTextContains(element, substr)
21. elementTextMatches(element, regex)

Below example illustrates how to wait until title of page becomes as expected.

```
var assert = require('assert');
var webdriver = require('selenium-webdriver'),
By = webdriver.By,
until = webdriver.until;

var chrome = require("selenium-
webdriver/chrome");
```

```
var options = new chrome.Options();
options.addArguments("start-maximized");
options.addArguments("test-type");
var driver = new webdriver.Builder().
withCapabilities(options.toCapabilities()).buil
d();


//Pageload time out of 50 seconds
driver.manage().timeouts().pageLoadTimeout(1000
*50);


//Implicit wait of 20 seconds
driver.manage().timeouts().implicitlyWait(1000*
20);


driver.get('http://www.softpost.org/selenium-
test-page/');


//For example - If you want to wait until title of
the page becomes say "Selenium Test Page", you can
use below syntax.
//Wait for 4 seconds for title to become
"Selenium Test Page | Free Software Tutorials"
driver.wait(until.titleIs('Selenium Test Page |
Free Software Tutorials'), 1000*4);


driver.getTitle().then(function(title) {
console.log("title is " + title);
assert(title==="Selenium Test Page | Free
Software Tutorials");
});


driver.quit();
```

Check if element exists on page

Below example illustrates how to check if an element exists in Selenium.

```
var assert = require('assert');
var webdriver = require('selenium-webdriver'),
By = webdriver.By,
until = webdriver.until;
var chrome = require("selenium-
webdriver/chrome");
var options = new chrome.Options();
options.addArguments("start-maximized");
options.addArguments("disable-popup-blocking");
options.addArguments("test-type");
var driver = new webdriver.Builder().
withCapabilities(options.toCapabilities()).buil
d();

//We can use below code block to check if element
exists on the webpage.

driver.get("http://www.softpost.org");

var webElements =
driver.findElements(By.id("myid"));

webElements.then(function (elements) {

if(elements.length==0)
console.log("Element myid not present");
else
console.log("Element myid present");
});

driver.quit();
```

12. Working with Tables using Selenium

In this topic, You will learn how to perform below operations on table using Selenium.

1. Find total number of rows and columns in a table
2. Read a value from the table cell
3. Click on elements inside table cells

Finding total number of rows and columns in a table

1. //table//tr - This XPATH can be used to get all tr elements inside the table. Note that if there are nested tables, it will get all nested tr elements as well. To get only immediate child tr elements, you will have to use children property which returns collection of child tr elements. Alternatively you can use "//table/tr" XPATH to find only immediate child tr elements. Note that we have used single / which means find only immediate children.
2. //table//th -This XPATH can be used to find total number of columns in a table. Note that all column headings should be marked with th tag. Also note that if one th tag spans multiple columns, it will be counted only once.
3. //table//tr[1]//td - This XPATH finds all td elements (table cells) in the first row of the table. Note that all nested td elements will be found using this XPATH expression.

Here is a simple example on Tables.

```
var tableCells =
driver.findElements(By.tagName("//table//td"));


tableCells .then(function (elements) {


console.log("Total number of cells -> " +
elements.length+ "\n");

//Print data from each cell
for (var i=0; i < elements.length; i++){
elements[i].getText().then(function(txt){
console.log(txt + "\n");
});
}
});
```

13. Performing advanced actions using Selenium in Node.js

We can below actions using ActionSequence.

1. Right click on the element
2. Drag and drop an element
3. Double click on an element
4. Simulating mouse over action

Below example illustrates how to perform actions in Selenium in Node.js

```
var assert = require('assert');
var webdriver = require('selenium-webdriver'),
By = webdriver.By,
until = webdriver.until;


var chrome = require("selenium-
webdriver/chrome");


var options = new chrome.Options();
options.addArguments("start-maximized");
options.addArguments("disable-popup-blocking");
options.addArguments("test-type");
var driver = new webdriver.Builder().
withCapabilities(options.toCapabilities()).buil
d();


driver.get('http://www.softpost.org/selenium-
test-page/');
var e3 =
driver.findElement(By.tagName('select'));

//You can use ActionSequence class to perform actions in selenium
```

```
new webdriver.ActionSequence(driver).
keyDown(webdriver.Key.SHIFT).
click(e3).
//dragAndDrop(element3, element4).
keyUp(webdriver.Key.SHIFT).
perform();


//In the same way, you can perform below actions.
//sendKeys, mouseUp , mouseMove, mouseDown,
dragAndDrop, doubleClick


driver.sleep(5000);


driver.quit();
//Similarly we can also do touch actions on mobile
phones
```

14. Executing JavaScript in Selenium in Node.js

Below example explains how to execute JavaScript in Selenium in Node.js

```
//You can execute the Java Script using below syntax.
var assert = require('assert');
var webdriver = require('selenium-webdriver'),
By = webdriver.By,
until = webdriver.until;


var chrome = require("selenium-webdriver/chrome");


var options = new chrome.Options();
var driver = new webdriver.Builder().
withCapabilities(options.toCapabilities()).buil
d();


driver.get('http://www.softpost.org/selenium-test-page/');


//simple javascript
driver.executeScript("return document.body.innerHTML;").then(function
(returnValue) {
console.log("Return Value ->" + returnValue);
});


//using javascript function
var myfunction = function () {
return document.body.innerHTML;
}
```

```
driver.executeScript(myfunction).then(function
(returnValue) {
console.log("Return Value by myfunction -> " +
returnValue);
});


//passing arguments to javascript function
var f1 = function (element) {
element.click();
}


var e1 =
driver.findElement(By.xpath("//input[@value='fe
male']"))
driver.executeScript(f1,e1).then(function
(returnValue) {
console.log("Return Value of f1 ->" +
returnValue);
});
driver.sleep(5000);


driver.findElement(By.id('fn')).sendKeys('Shaun
');


//Returning value from javascript function
var f2 = function (element) {
return element.value;
}


var e2 = driver.findElement(By.id('fn'));
driver.executeScript(f2,e2).then(function
(returnValue) {
console.log("Return Value of f2 ->" +
returnValue);
});
driver.quit();
```

15. Switching contexts

15.1 Working with multiple Browser Windows or tabs

Below example illustrates how to work multiple browser windows or tabs in Selenium.

```
var assert = require('assert');
var webdriver = require('selenium-webdriver'),
By = webdriver.By,
until = webdriver.until;


var chrome = require("selenium-
webdriver/chrome");


var options = new chrome.Options();
options.addArguments("start-maximized");
options.addArguments("disable-popup-blocking");
options.addArguments("test-type");
var driver = new webdriver.Builder().
withCapabilities(options.toCapabilities()).buil
d();
driver.get('http://www.softpost.org/selenium-
test-page/');


//To get the window handle, you can use
getWindowHandle method.
driver.getWindowHandle().then(function
(mainWindowHandle) {
console.log ("Main window handle is " +
mainWindowHandle);


var e1 =
driver.findElement(By.partialLinkText('Selenium
in Java'));
driver.executeScript(f1,e1);
driver.getAllWindowHandles().then(function
```

```
(windowHandles) {
console.log("Total number of windows " +
windowHandles.length);
//Here you can switch to the another window using
windowHandles variable
windowHandles.forEach(function(handle){
console.log(handle + "\n");
if(!(handle===mainWindowHandle))
{
//Switch to new browser window
console.log("Switching to other window");
driver.switchTo().window(handle);
driver.getTitle().then(function (title) {
console.log("Title of new window -> " + title);
});
}
});
});


//Switch to original window
driver.switchTo().window(mainWindowHandle);
driver.getTitle().then(function (title) {
console.log("Title of original window -> " +
title);
});
});


//Below function is used to click on the element
using native javascript in browser
var f1 = function (element) {
element.click();
}

driver.quit();
```

15.2 Working with multiple frames

Below example illustrates how to switch to frames in Selenium in Node.js

```
var assert = require('assert');
var webdriver = require('selenium-webdriver'),
By = webdriver.By,
until = webdriver.until;

var chrome = require("selenium-
webdriver/chrome");

var options = new chrome.Options();
options.addArguments("start-maximized");
options.addArguments("test-type");
var driver = new webdriver.Builder().
withCapabilities(options.toCapabilities()).buil
d();

driver.get('http://www.softpost.org/selenium-
test-page/');

/*
We can use below code to switch to default
content.
driver.switchTo().defaultContent();
*/
driver.switchTo().frame("g");
driver.getPageSource().then(function (source) {
console.log("HTML Source of frame -> " +
source);
});

driver.sleep(5000);

driver.switchTo().defaultContent();
driver.getPageSource().then(function (source) {
```

```
console.log("HTML Source of main page -> " +
source);
});
driver.quit();
```

15.3 Handling alerts

Below example explains how to work with alerts in
Selenium in Node.js

```
var assert = require('assert');
var webdriver = require('selenium-webdriver'),
By = webdriver.By,
until = webdriver.until;

var chrome = require("selenium-
webdriver/chrome");

var options = new chrome.Options();
options.addArguments("start-maximized");
options.addArguments("test-type");
var driver = new webdriver.Builder().
withCapabilities(options.toCapabilities()).buil
d();

//We can use below code to click on Ok button
on alert dialog.
driver.switchTo().alert().accept();

//We can use below code to click on cancel
button on alert dialog.
driver.switchTo().alert().dismiss();
```

16. Common exceptions in Selenium

You may encounter below types of exceptions and errors when working with Selenium in Node.js

1. Element is not clickable at point ....This exception comes when Selenium is not able to click on the element as it is hidden or wrapped in other html tag. To fix this issue, you need to use native JavaScript click method.
2. No Such Element.....This exception comes when element is not found in the web page matching given locator. To prevent this exception, make sure that you have given correct xpath, css selector. Also make sure that element actually exists on the page.
3. The path to the driver executable must be set by the webdriver.chrome.driver system property........This error comes when driver exe file is not found in the system Path or in JVM argument. To fix this issue, you need to make sure that exe file is present in system path.
4. Stale Element Exception - This exception comes when you try to access the element which is loaded afresh in the page. To fix this issue, you need to call findElement method to get the reference to fresh element.
5. IE issues - When trying to launch the IE browser, you may encounter error saying protected mode settings are not same for all security zones. To prevent this issue, you need to make sure that protected mode settings are same for all zones in IE.

17. Frameworks in Selenium

17.1 Taking a screenshot in selenium

Below example illustrates how to take a screenshot in Selenium in Node.js

```
var assert = require('assert');
var fs = require('fs');
var webdriver = require('selenium-webdriver'),
By = webdriver.By,
until = webdriver.until;


var chrome = require("selenium-
webdriver/chrome");


var options = new chrome.Options();
options.addArguments("start-maximized");
options.addArguments("test-type");
var driver = new webdriver.Builder().
withCapabilities(options.toCapabilities()).buil
d();


driver.get('http://www.softpost.org/selenium-
test-page/');
//You can use below code to take the Screenshot
of the web page.


driver.takeScreenshot().then(
function(image, err) {
//Screenshot will be saved under current
directory with name myscreenshot.png
fs.writeFile('myscreenshot.png', image,
'base64', function(error) {
if(error!=null)
console.log("Error occured while saving
screenshot" + error);
});
```

```
}
);

driver.quit();
```

17.2 Mocha - Unit testing framework

Just like how we have JUnit and TestNG testing frameworks in Java world, we have a mocha (https://mochajs.org/) framework in node.js

You can use below command to install mocha package.
npm install mocha

//Below example shows how to use testing framework in node.js

```
var assert = require('assert');

var webdriver = require('selenium-webdriver'),
By = webdriver.By,
until = webdriver.until;

var test = require('selenium-
webdriver/testing');

var chrome = require("selenium-
webdriver/chrome");

//Describe is equivalent to the test class in
JUnit
test.describe('Verify the title of the Page',
function() {
this.timeout(30*1000);
var driver;
```

```
//before is equivalent to the @before
annotation in JUnit
test.before(function() {
var options = new chrome.Options();
options.addArguments("start-maximized");
options.addArguments("test-type");
driver = new
webdriver.Builder().withCapabilities(options.to
Capabilities()).build();


});


//"it" is equivalent to the @test annotation in
JUnit
test.it('Title should be equal to Selenium Test
Page | Free Software Tutorials', function() {
driver.get('http://www.softpost.org/selenium-
test-page/');
driver.wait(until.titleIs('Selenium Test Page |
Free Software Tutorials'), 4000);
driver.getTitle().then(function(title) {
console.log("title is " + title);
assert(title=='Selenium Test Page | Free
Software Tutorials');
});


});


//after is equivalent to the @after annotation
in JUnit
test.after(function() {
driver.quit();
});


});
```

To run the tests, we can use below syntax.
mocha s1.js

We can put all test files in "test" directory and then run all
tests in test directory using below command.

```
mocha
```

You may get below error if you try to run the js file
containing mocha tests using node command.
node mochatests.js
c:\selenium-node\node_modules\selenium-
webdriver\testing\index.js:226
exports.describe.skip = global.describe.skip; ^
TypeError: Cannot read property 'skip' of undefined
*/

18. Selenium grid

You can also use standalone server to run your tests. Just start the server using below command.

java -jar selenium-server-standalone.jar

By default server (Hub) starts running at
http://localhost:4444/wd/hub

//To connect to Grid, you will have to use below syntax.

```
var assert = require('assert');
var webdriver = require('selenium-webdriver'),
By = webdriver.By,
until = webdriver.until;

var chrome = require("selenium-
webdriver/chrome");

var driver = new webdriver.Builder()
.forBrowser('chrome')
.usingServer('http://localhost:4444/wd/hub')
.build();

driver.get("http://www.softpost.org");

driver.quit();
```

You can use below command to run tests on grid.
//SELENIUM_REMOTE_URL="http://localhost:4444/wd/hu
b" node yourscript.js